MOUNTAIN CLIMBING

Scaling the Heights

by Monica Devine

Perfection Learning®

Cover Photo
of Mt. McKinley: Steve McCutcheon
Inside Illustration: Kay Ewald

About the Author

Monica Devine is a speech-language pathologist and freelance writer
who resides in Eagle River, Alaska. She has traveled extensively throughout
Alaskan villages, working with Yupik and Inupiaq Eskimo families with
special needs. She is the author of *Growing Together: Communication
Activities for Infants and Toddlers, Baby Talk,* and *The Iditarod: The
Greatest Win Ever.*

Monica is an avid photographer and outdoor enthusiast. With her
husband and two sons, she enjoys all that Alaska has to offer: skijoring and
following the Iditarod Sled Dog Race in the winter and backpacking,
bicycling, and fishing in the summer.

Table of Contents

The Mountain with Two Names 5

Chapter 1. Denali, the High One 7

Chapter 2. Safety First 13

Chapter 3. Climbing Stronger 19

Chapter 4. Waiting It Out 26

Chapter 5. Summit Fever 35

Chapter 6. To the Top 45

Appendix 56

Glossary 61

Index 64

The Mountain with Two Names

Mt. McKinley is the highest mountain in North America. At 20,320 feet, it towers over all the others in the Alaska Range. Every year, climbers from all over the world try to reach its summit. Some make it. Others don't. Some die trying.

Alaskans called the mountain *Denali,* which means "The High One" or "The Great One." In the late 1800s, a gold digger in Alaska told others about the mountain. He renamed the mountain in honor of William McKinley, the twenty-fifth president of the U.S. Most Alaskans still call the mountain Denali.

There are several different climbing routes to the top of Denali. The most popular is called the **West Buttress.** Climbers fly from the small Alaskan town of Talkeetna to the Kahiltna Glacier.

The Kahiltna Glacier is about ⅓ of the way to the top of Denali. It is at 7,200 feet.

The Kahiltna Glacier serves as a starting-off point for those climbing the West Buttress. Small planes with skis deliver the climbers.

But the glacier pilots can't always fly when they want to. Fierce snowstorms are common, even during the summer months. The weather is always changing on Denali.

To reach the summit is a great honor. One no climber will ever forget.

Mt. McKinley and the Kahiltna Glacier
Photo by Steve McCutcheon

WEST BUTTRESS OF MT. McKINLEY

- **1** Kahiltna Glacier
- **2** Ski Hill
- **3** Kahiltna Pass   10,320'
- **4** Motorcycle Hill   11,500'
- **5** Windy Corner   13,200'
- **6** Headwall
- **7** 17,200'
- **8** Denali Pass   18,200'
- **9** Football Field   19,600'
- **10** Summit   20,320'

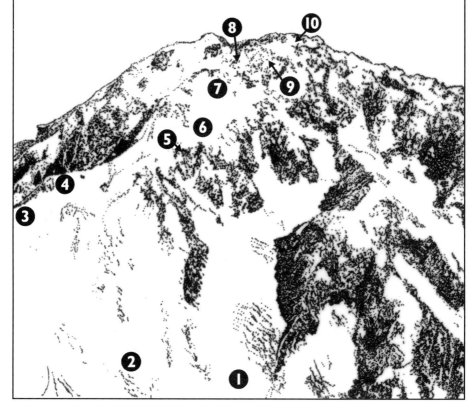

CHAPTER 1

Denali, the High One

Jason rolled up his sleeping bag. Then he stuffed it into his backpack. He had spent two days on the Kahiltna **Glacier.** Finally, he and his team were ready to start climbing.

Jason thought back two days. It had been a green June day when he boarded the plane in Talkeetna. Forty minutes later, he was on the mighty mountain of Denali.

Jason peeked outside the tent. The sky was gray and foggy. He couldn't see the **summit** of Denali. But the weather was beginning to clear.

Jason knew it could take two to three weeks to reach the summit. It all depended on the weather. He hoped there wouldn't be any storms.

"Maybe you'll make it home by your birthday," his mother had said. But who could think about birthdays now. He just wanted to start climbing.

Still, Jason had come prepared to wait out storms. He had three books to read. One was about Barry Sanders, the greatest running back in NFL history. He also had a murder mystery. It was about the death of a World Cup soccer player.

He couldn't remember what the third book was. His girlfriend, Stephanie, had stuffed it into his backpack at the airstrip.

Jason heard his dad, Frank, outside the tent. Frank was talking with Kelly, the assistant guide.

*"We'll **cache** our snowshoes and sleds at 11,000 feet,"* Kelly said. *"Then we'll put **crampons** on our boots and carry our backpacks the rest of the way up.*

"It's a long climb. We'll be hauling our supplies up bit by bit. We'll climb about 1,000 feet and cache some supplies. Then we'll climb back down for the rest."

*"What about doing it **alpine style?"** Jason's dad asked. "No sleds. We can just carry everything in our backpacks. It'll take less time."*

"Sure, it'll take less time. But it's risky," Kelly added. *"Your body has to get used to being up so high. So you don't get **mountain sickness.** You need the time.*

"The higher you go, the less oxygen there is," Kelly went on. *"Some days, we'll just stay in camp and rest. Moving slowly will help us adjust to the thin air."*

"I see what you mean," Frank replied.

"Well, it looks like the fog is starting to lift," Kelly said. *"It's time to get climbing."*

Jason finished packing his sled. Then he strapped on his snowshoes and yanked his ski poles out of the snow.

The wait was over. The five climbers began their **ascent.** Jason felt a stir of excitement.

Jason was the only kid on the team. And kids don't usually climb Denali. That had made him feel uneasy at first.

But he wasn't the only one to stand out. There was Kelly. She was the only girl on the team.

Jason admired Kelly. She had lots of climbing experience. Besides climbing other peaks around the world, she had climbed Denali three times before.

Jason pulled his harness around his waist and hips. He cinched it in front with a **carabiner** and threaded the safety rope through.

"Jason, make sure that rope is taut," Dean called.

Dean was the head guide. He made sure everyone was **roped up** correctly. Jason felt secure with him. After all, Dean had made it to the summit six times. He knew mighty Denali well.

Behind Dean was Kenny, a hotshot climber from Washington state. Kenny wore a purple bandanna around his head. His pockets were packed with candy bars.

Jason smiled to himself. What an interesting group! he thought.

The climbers walked up the long, wide glacier. They skirted a large **crevasse** to their left.

ROPES AND TEAMWORK

Crevasses are slits or big holes in a glacier. They can be hundreds of feet deep.

Most of the time, climbers can see crevasses. Then they snowshoe around them.

But sometimes crevasses are hidden by loose snow. That's why all climbers must be roped up.

Climbers wear harnesses around their waists and thighs. The harnesses are held together in front with large metal loops called *carabiners*. The rope is threaded through each climber's carabiner. The team is then roped up in a long, straight line.

If a climber falls into a crevasse, the others drop to the ground at once. Their weight pulls the rope taut. This breaks the climber's fall. Then the others can pull the climber out of the hole safely.

Some climbers wear a chest harness as an added safety measure. The chest harness prevents a fallen climber from tipping upside down. Imagine dangling upside down wearing a 40-pound backpack!

Before setting up camp, climbers check for covered crevasses. They probe, or poke, the snow with a wand. Then the boundaries of the camp are marked with orange wands.

Once a camp is marked, the team can unrope. The climbers are free to move around camp. But not beyond the camp's borders.

Jason looked over the lip. He marveled at the long, narrow hole in the snow. He couldn't tell how deep it was because he couldn't see the bottom.

The sun sparkled on the snow. Still the ice in the crevasse was blue. Deep and blue and beautiful.

Like a line of ants, the climbers trudged uphill. One snowshoe in front of the other. Slowly, carefully, they climbed.

Jason carried 30 pounds of gear in his pack and 25 pounds on the sled. After a few hours, his legs and hips ached.

Jason stripped off his pile jacket. With the sun reflecting off the snow, the temperature was near 60°.

"Remember, drink lots of water," Dean announced. "Three to four quarts a day.

"If you don't, you're an easy target for **dehydration,"** Dean continued. "Even if you don't feel thirsty . . . drink."

Jason unscrewed the cap of his water bottle. He took long, deep swigs. Kenny offered him a candy bar.

"Hey, guys," Kenny said. "We haven't picked a name for our expedition. Every climbing team has to have a name."

"How about the Water Bellies?" Jason said. "My stomach feels like it's sloshing around right now."

"Naw," Dean said. "How about the Mountain Sun Expedition?" He tilted his face into the sunlight.

"I like Obsession," said Kelly.

"That sounds like a perfume," said Frank.

"It's like naming a baby," Frank added. "You have to wait and get to know it a little better before you name it."

After snacks of bagels, **gorp,** and plenty of water, they roped up again. Jason felt better. The snacks and water energized him for more climbing.

✥✥✥

By early evening, the team reached 7,500 feet. They cached food and fuel and headed back down the glacier.

The hike down was easy and fast. Carrying the second load of supplies up was easier too.

After a long, hard day, they set up camp. Everyone had a job to do.

Dean probed the snow all around, looking for crevasses. Then he marked the outside of the camp with orange wands.

"Remember, stay inside the camp boundaries," Dean said. "Inside the wands, there are no crevasses. Always think safety."

Jason and Kelly pulled out the food bags. Chocolate chip cookies, banana bread, meat, noodles, vegetables, oatmeal, and candy bars.

Jason was starving. He didn't know what to eat first.

"Eat up. You need 4,000 calories a day," Kelly said.

"No problem. No problem at all," Jason said as he bit into a hunk of cheddar cheese.

Frank and Kenny put up tents. They stomped down the snow and made two platforms.

Jason and his dad claimed the yellow tent. Kenny, Kelly, and Dean shared the larger orange tent.

After a hot meal, Jason rubbed his sore muscles. Climbing back and forth was hard work. And Jason's body ached all over.

After a short rest, the team continued their climb up the long, wide glacier. Since it was summer in Alaska, the skies never got completely dark at night. So the team traveled whenever they wanted. Sometimes they rested during the day and traveled at night.

Jason quickly lost track of what day it was. And even whether it was night or day. He was so busy climbing, he forgot about everything. Even his girlfriend, Stephanie.

CHAPTER 2

Safety First

The next day brought clear, sunny skies. The team slept until midday. Then they lazed around camp. The night before, they had climbed for eight hours. So everyone was tired.

Frank and Jason exchanged back rubs before crawling out of their tent. "Let's get a meal going," Frank said. "Everyone's up and around."

"And probably starving," Jason added.

They fired up the stoves to melt snow. Jason and Frank worked in T-shirts.

The sun was bright. Its glare stung Jason's eyes. So he put on his glacier goggles.

Jason stirred the soup pot. He loved the warm feel of the sun on his arms and face.

Suddenly, the silence was broken.

"H-e-l-l-l-l-p-p-p!"

Jason spun around. For an instant, he saw Kenny's arms flail in the air, then disappear.

"Help, help!" Kenny cried again.

"What happened?" Dean shouted.

"I think Kenny fell into a crevasse," Jason yelled.

Dean called out orders. "Frank, bring the ropes."

"Kelly, the snow shovel."

"Jason, a sled and first aid."

"Follow behind me. We don't know how far the crevasse extends. I'll have to probe."

Dean carried a long orange wand and probed in front of him. Carefully, he punched the wand into the snow. He took one step at a time.

Slowly, the others followed behind him. They stopped short of the hole that had swallowed Kenny.

Kenny lay trembling on a snow cliff about twenty feet down. Six inches beyond his boots, the crevasse tumbled down, down, down. Black rock and blue ice jutted up from below.

"Kenny, I'm sending down a rope," Dean shouted.

"I'm so cold," Kenny's weak voice shook. He rubbed his bare arms. His harness was still clipped around his thighs.

Dean fed down a rope with a carabiner clipped to the end. "Clip the carabiner onto your harness," Dean called. "Then we can pull you up."

"I . . . I . . . I . . . can't." The deep cold slowed Kenny's motions and his speech. It was like being in a freezer, bare-armed. He was shivering.

"Kenny," Dean shouted. "YOU MUST CLIP INTO THE ROPE . . . NOW!"

Kenny moved slowly. He tried to stand up, but he didn't have enough room on the narrow shelf of snow.

Kenny's hands fumbled at the rope dangling in front of him. He grabbed once and missed. He grabbed again. Missed. After a third try, he got it. He held it firmly in his cold, fisted hands.

"Okay, now clip it into your harness," Dean coached.

"I . . . I . . ." Suddenly, Kenny's hands dropped to his waist. His fists opened. The rope swung free.

"Kenny!" Dean shouted. "You must try again. Take the rope. Come on, you can do it."

Kenny's teeth were chattering. He swung at the rope, now with fisted hands. It dangled in front of his face.

"Come on, Kenny. One more try," Dean insisted. "YOU MUST GRAB THE ROPE!"

Dean dangled the rope within inches of Kenny's fingers. Kenny flung out his arm. He pressed the rope tightly against his chest. His hands were still fisted.

Slowly, he slid his arm down the rope. He opened his fingers and wrapped them around the rope.

"Okay. Good work," Dean coaxed. "Now the clip. Clip the rope to your harness."

In slow motion, Kenny clipped the rope to his harness.

Dean wasted no time. He placed a snow shovel under the rope at the lip of the hole. "We don't want the rope to cut into the snow as we pull," he said. "One, two, three—pull."

Everyone pulled. Kenny was hoisted up and out.

"Let's get some hot liquid into him right away," Dean instructed. "How are you doing, Kenny?"

"I'll . . . be . . . okay," he said weakly.

Dean helped him into a long underwear shirt and a pile jacket. His color was beginning to look better. He was slowly warming.

The climbers followed their footprints in the snow back to camp. Frank pulled Jason aside.

"NEVER, EVER, <u>EVER</u> walk around outside of camp unroped," Frank said angrily.

Jason looked up at his dad. "I know that. Why are you yelling at me?"

"Dean has told us a hundred times," Frank continued. "And still, you saw what happened."

"Dad, I didn't walk around outside of camp," Jason said.

"It could have been you," Frank said and walked away.

Spirits were broken. The mood in camp was grim. Kenny's accident had frightened everyone.

After camp chores, the climbers walked to their tents in silence. Jason stayed outside. He didn't feel like being alone with his dad.

Jason sat on a gear bag and watched clouds move across the sky.

Why did I let Dad talk me into this trip anyway? Jason thought. He's the one that wants to make it to the top. All he does is yell at me. Expecting me to be Mr. Perfect. Jason was so angry he felt like crying.

As far back as he could remember, Jason had admired Denali from afar. On a clear day, they could see Denali from their home in Eagle River. He and his dad had agreed that someday they would climb it together.

But Jason hadn't thought it would turn out like this. He wanted to have fun. Be friends. Not fight.

Jason ran the accident through his mind again. He couldn't stop thinking about it. Kenny could have frozen to death in that hole.

Jason wanted to be home with Stephanie. And off this crazy mountain.

The team rested for another six hours. No one said much about the accident, except Dean.

"Kenny should have known better," Dean said. "He needs to humble himself and become friends again with the mountain."

Kenny himself was quieter than before, more thoughtful. Probably more than anything, he was embarrassed by his mistake. A mistake that could have cost him his life.

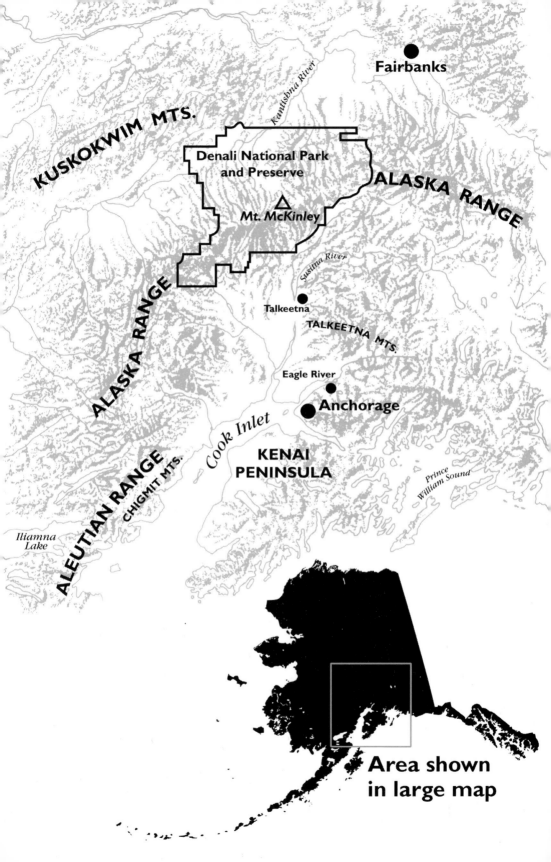

KUSKOKWIM MTS.

Kantishna River

Fairbanks

Denali National Park
and Preserve

ALASKA RANGE

△
Mt. McKinley

ALASKA RANGE

Susitna River

Talkeetna

TALKEETNA MTS.

Eagle River
Anchorage

Cook Inlet

KENAI
PENINSULA

*Prince
William Sound*

ALEUTIAN RANGE

CHIGMIT MTS.

*Iliamna
Lake*

Area shown
in large map

CHAPTER 3

Climbing Stronger

Jason woke up groggy. He had tossed and turned all night.

Kenny was fully recovered, and it was time to break camp. The climbers did their chores and roped up. Jason was roped between Kelly and his dad.

"This next section is steep, so be very careful," warned Dean. "Today we climb to 10,000 feet, maybe 11. If the weather's good."

Then Dean gave his usual daily lecture about safety. Everyone paid a little more attention this time.

Jason lacked energy. His shoulders ached. His pack felt heavy.

As Jason plodded up Ski Hill, his sled swished behind him. Low clouds clung to the mountain. He couldn't see the summit. Maybe that's why he felt so down.

Jason looked all around. All he could see were gray clouds drooping next to the **rockface**. Black rock bleeding through the clouds. Black and gray. Black and white.

Jason thought of home. Only forty minutes away, it's June green. People hoeing in their gardens. Orange and yellow poppies lining the roadside. Nothing grows up here in this cold, harsh place, he thought.

Step by step, they plodded along. Slowly but steadily. Jason planted his ski poles carefully to keep his balance.

The snow was soft and mushy. Jason's snowshoes felt awkward on the long, steep hill. Too bad we aren't using skis, Jason thought. It sure would be fun skiing down this part of the mountain.

Sweat dripped into Jason's eyes. Every step was hard work. Just like in football practice. Only worse.

He thought about football. What a great season. 10 and 0.

But the last game had been rough. A tackle by a 190-pound defensive end had left Jason with a torn knee ligament.

After the injury, Jason worried about the climb. Not to mention next year's training.

He had worked hard to build up his knee—swimming and cross-country skiing.

And all the training had paid off. His knee wasn't bothering him on this hard climb. Plus, now he'd be stronger for next year's football season.

Jason turned and watched his dad. Frank was a strong athlete. Still, he had to stop often and catch his breath.

The group stopped for drinks and snacks midway up. A misty fog began to close in. The Kahiltna Pass was near. But not in view because of the fog.

Kenny handed out candy bars. Kelly and Dean munched on beef jerky while discussing the route.

"We'll be moving even slower," Dean said. "With such low fog, I can't see far enough ahead to judge the route."

Along the way, Dean had marked the trail with orange wands. This would ensure a safe route on the way back down. As long as the wind didn't blow the wands down.

"We'll take it real slow until the fog lifts," Dean told everyone. "You're all doing a great job. Just hang in there. And remember, drink, drink, drink.

"You're sweating and losing fluid," Dean continued. "So drink even when you don't feel like it."

Ugh. More water, Jason thought. He emptied a pack of red Kool-Aid into his water bottle. Cherry sweet. He had saved it for long, hard climbs.

CARRYING AND CACHING GEAR

Climbing teams can either ski or snowshoe up to the 11,000-foot level. The less-experienced teams use snowshoes. They also use ski poles to keep their balance. Other more-experienced climbers use skis.

Each climber carries a backpack. It is stuffed with gear. It can weigh anywhere from 30 to 50 pounds.

The climber also pulls a sled hooked by a rope to his harness. The sled carries food, tents, fuel, and other gear.

At 11,000 feet, the team leaves behind their sleds, ski poles, and snowshoes. From there, the climb gets steeper. The climbers continue to cache supplies. They carry food and fuel up, bury it in the snow, and then go back down to bring up more.

Fierce storms are very common on the mountain. Extra food and fuel is needed in case the climbers get stormed-in for days at a time.

From 11,000 feet to the summit, the climb changes. It is colder and the snow is often wind-hardened. The climbers wear boots with crampons, or "foot fangs." Crampons are metal frames with spikes that are attached to the boots. The spikes dig into the snow and ice and give the climber traction. For balance, the climber uses his ice ax as a walking stick on the steeper sections.

Hours passed. Jason was in his zone—that place where you aren't thinking of anything. You feel hypnotized. Doing the same thing over and over and over.

He climbed. One snowshoe in front of the other. Nothing to look at but white snow and gray fog.

Jason's neck ached from looking down so long. He rubbed his eyes and forehead. He looked up and saw small patches of blue through the fog.

"About one hundred more feet," Dean called.

Jason lifted his head. One hundred? No sweat. His step lightened.

Everyone picked up their pace. Finally they crested the ridge and rose above the fog. Deep, blue sky encircled them.

"Wow! We're at 10,000 feet! Yeoooww!" Jason shouted.

"Yeah, and we've got ten thousand more to go," Frank added. "And the hardest part is yet to come."

Jason hated how his dad could so easily burst his bubble. Why can't he just be happy about where we are now? he wondered.

"We've come a long way," Dean said. "We should be able to go back down and bring up supplies much quicker. Now that the trail is marked."

Kenny melted snow and started water for hot drinks. In another pot, he dumped noodles, onions, spices, rice, and meat. He worked quickly.

"Wow! That smells good," Jason said. "I'm starving."

"Yeah, we'll eat hearty today," Kenny said. "Once we cache everything, we'll be climbing with just our backpacks. No more heavy meat and cheese to carry. It'll be light freeze-dried foods only. And candy bars, of course."

Jason smiled. He was glad Kenny's sense of humor had returned.

"Ya know, it's funny up here," Jason said. "Seems like the

sky is either crystal clear. Or it's so foggy, you can't see a thing. Not many partly cloudy days."

"Yeah. And you have to pay attention to the weather on this mountain," Kenny said. "All the time. You have to notice the clouds. Understand what they mean. Especially closer to the summit.

"One general climbing rule is never try to reach the summit when there are **lenticulars,**" Kenny continued. "Lenticular clouds mean very high winds. Winds up to 100 mph. That kind of weather can uproot tents and send them shooting into the sky like kites. Or lift a person off his feet. Blow him right off the mountain."

Lenticular clouds

24

Not a problem today, Jason thought as he faced the glowing afternoon sun. It had turned into a perfect day. The weather was clear and sunny.

The group worked as a unit. They set up camp quickly and efficiently. We've become a real team, Jason thought.

The sun slowly arched across the sky. Jason felt strong. Like after a hard-fought game. His muscles ached faintly from the day's climb. But he wasn't in pain. What a workout! Compared to this, football training was a piece of cake.

~·§·~·§·~

Jason awoke at 4 a.m. to the sound of pans clanging. He peered outside the tent. Another blue sky day. Was this luck or what?

"Hey, sleepyhead!" Frank called. "Come out and see this view."

Jason laughed. Everyone's in a good mood when the skies are blue, he thought.

The night before, he had removed his boots to air out his feet. Now his toes stung in the cold, biting air. It was chillier than the night before. A light wind was blowing.

Jason layered on clothing—a wool sweater and a pile jacket over his long underwear. Two pairs of socks and his boots. A light pair of gloves covered with overmitts.

Jason stood with the others, admiring the view. "Finally, the mountain's out!" he said.

The summit ridge of Denali was bathed in **alpenglow,** a pink and golden hue. In the distance, a quarter moon was sinking as the midnight sun rose. The air was silent.

"Stephanie, I wish you could see this," Jason whispered. "Denali is truly awesome."

CHAPTER 4

Waiting It Out

The rest of the day the climbers did nothing.

"We have to get used to being up this high. We don't want anyone getting mountain sickness. So enjoy your day, and we'll head out tonight," Dean said.

There were a few camp chores to do. So Jason got right to work. He couldn't sit still. It was too beautiful. Too awesome. He danced around camp.

Kelly was reading a paperback. Kenny and Dean relaxed in the sun.

Back in the tent, Frank wrote in his journal. He took notes of their progress every day.

We've climbed to Kahiltna Pass, at 10,320 feet. The team is doing great. Sunshine and blue skies. The summit awaits us . . .

Jason didn't take any notes. Most of the day he spent reading or playing on a small chessboard with Kenny. Or thinking about Stephanie. Or football.

They'd been on the mountain for five days, but it felt like much longer. Probably because they moved slowly—for safety's sake.

By 8 p.m., everyone had eaten, written in journals, played chess, and read books. They'd even slept. Dean's orders.

Finally, it was time to move on.

The night air was quiet and cold. Dean kept the pace slow to prevent **exhaustion.** He wanted to gain no more than 1,000 feet per day. "Safe and slow" was his motto.

Jason was glad they were moving slowly. Traveling with a heavy pack and sled was no picnic.

Once they were climbing again, Jason wondered if it was worth all this hard work. He had never put this much effort into anything before. He noticed how his mood changed with the weather.

Denali has moods too, Jason thought. Some days, she allows you to climb. Other days, you're not so lucky. In the end, Denali has the last word.

The team pushed on. The snow was crisp and hard. Jason had to pound his snowshoes to get a good grip.

The climbers passed through a **crevasse field**. Large gaping holes in the snow that could swallow you alive. Jason tried to focus his mind on other things.

"Rest stop. Motorcycle Hill," Dean announced. "How's everybody doing?"

"Great. I'm ready to jump on my Harley and gun it right up the mountain," Kenny said. Everyone chuckled.

It had been a quiet, productive night. After a hot meal, Jason still wasn't ready to sleep. He suddenly had a burst of energy. A second wind.

"Do you guys want something useful to do?" Dean asked Jason. "You and your dad can start digging the cache."

He handed them two snow shovels. "We need to cache our snowshoes, ski poles, and enough food for our team. Just in case we get caught in a storm on the way back down. Happy digging."

Jason was eager for something to do. He wanted to stay active. So his muscles wouldn't get stiff and ache. Like if he skipped a day of football training. It was always hard to get back into it.

They dug in, hurling blocks of snow over their shoulders. Jason felt good working side by side with his dad.

This climb was his dad's dream, but it was his dream too. And now it was coming true.

"Make sure you dig deep enough," Dean warned. "Those darn ravens are real scavengers. They'll eat anything."

"And they do a good job of trashing supplies," Dean continued. "I've seen them up as high as 16,000 feet, tearing into food caches left too close to the surface."

Frank marked the cache after they were finished digging and burying their supplies. He taped two wands together to make one long one. He stuck it into the mound of snow. Then he marked it clearly with the leader's name and the date.

The next day, the team repacked their backpacks. No more sleds. They kept all the important items on their backs. Sleeping bags, two tents, food, extra clothing, a paperback book or two, rope, ice axes, and two snow shovels.

"Time for foot fangs," Dean announced. "Make sure they're strapped on tight. But not so tight that they squeeze your feet. The snow's hard up here. You'll really need them."

One type of the "foot fang" style of crampons

They roped up, with Jason between Kelly and Kenny. Jason felt light and strong as they moved along. He was glad to be rid of the awkward old snowshoes.

The snow at this level was crusty and firm. They moved at a swift pace. But they took frequent breaks for water and snacks.

Gusts of wind swirled light snow in front of Jason's face. He stopped to regain his balance.

"Kelly. Kenny. Stop," Jason called. "Check this out."

They stopped and viewed the mountains all around. At the base of the glaciers were miles and miles of **tundra.**

Rivers cut through the tundra like tiny cracks in a windshield. Jason imagined throwing a rock down. Just to see how it landed. "Anything dropped from this high wouldn't quit rolling for another 2,000 feet," he said.

The team trudged on. The wind was getting stronger. Jason hunched forward as he walked. They continued along the ridge for several more hours.

At the end of the ridge, a wide, windswept plateau came into view. "How is everybody doing?" Dean asked.

Jason looked around. Everyone looked weary.

"I have a terrible headache," Frank said. "I . . . I'm feeling pretty weak."

"I'm scouting for a campsite," Dean said. "Eat and drink as much as you can now, Frank. We'll stop as soon as we can."

The wind rose to a scream. It battered Jason's wind suit and blew snowy mini-tornadoes around him.

Jason was getting scared. He couldn't hear Kelly's voice ahead of him.

The group huddled together in the wind. "We're staying put," Dean said. "We can't move safely in this storm."

"Kelly and I will wand the area to mark out a campsite," Dean continued. "After that, we'll get the tents up. We'll have to build snow walls to buffet this wind."

The top layer of snow was hard and crusty. Jason chopped blocks out of the snow with a snow shovel. Kenny stacked the blocks on top of one another.

The wind howled as they worked. Blowing snow stung their faces. Frank slowly set up and anchored the tents. Soon they had formed a semicircle of blocks around the tents.

"This mountain is so massive, it creates its own storms." Dean struggled to close the tent flap. Outside the wind continued to scream.

"There's nothing we can do now," said Dean, "except wait. And try to sleep."

The wind blasted the tent. It was hard to hear each other speak.

Jason finished the Kool-Aid in his water bottle and lay back in his sleeping bag. His body ached all over. It had been a very long day. All he could think of was sleep. In fact, he didn't care if he ever reached the summit. He just wanted to sleep.

"No sleeping," Kelly told Jason. "You've got to eat first." She dumped a bag full of freeze-dried pasta, vegetables, and chicken into the **glop pot.**

Where does she get all her energy? Jason wondered.

"The higher we go, the more calories we burn," she said. "You'll be burning calories even while you sleep."

Kelly was happy after everyone stuffed themselves. The wind continued at a steady howl for four more hours.

Jason thought the constant roar would make him go crazy. But after a long time, he was finally able to tune it out. He fell into a deep, deep sleep.

When he awoke hours later, the wind was still howling.

"Well, it looks like we're stuck here," Dean said. "It figures. They call this area Windy Corner."

"Gee, I wonder why?" said Frank.

Jason stepped out into the wind. Another tent day. He couldn't see up. He couldn't see down. The blowing snow caused a **whiteout** all around him.

All Jason wanted to do was climb. But today they were stuck in tents.

By midday, Jason was bored. He finished reading the biography of Barry Sanders. He reorganized his backpack. He even beat his dad in two games of chess. That was a first. He had never beaten his dad in chess before.

"Dad, are you okay?" Jason asked. "You seem pretty down."

"I'm okay, I guess. I just can't get rid of this headache. Even aspirin isn't helping," Frank answered. "Don't worry, though. I'll be fine." He massaged his temples.

Jason heard someone outside their tent. He turned and unzipped the door.

"Can we come in?" Kenny, Kelly, and Dean squirmed in and sat down. There was barely enough room for all five of them.

"I wanted to talk to everyone about what to expect next," Dean said. Everyone huddled together.

"Once this storm clears, we'll head up to 14,200 feet. As you know, there's a camp there set up by the U.S. Park Service. In a way, sitting out this storm is a blessing. It gives our bodies more time to adjust to the **altitude,**" Dean continued.

"And if your body says stop, then you must STOP. We're only as strong as our weakest member. Understand?

"But most importantly, safety first. We don't want any accidents," Dean finished.

Everyone nodded.

"Speaking of accidents, I wanted to explain mine. I know I gave everybody a scare," Kenny said. "Myself included."

He continued. "I saw a yellow warbler just outside the camp's boundary. It was perched on a mound of snow, singing.

"I'd never seen a bird up that high before. Usually they can't find food. And they freeze to death.

"But that yellow songbird was going to make it," Kenny continued. "He was going to make it through the shadow of Denali.

"I didn't see any crevasses, so I wandered a few more feet out. Figured I'd get a closer look. Then I fell." Kenny

Yellow warbler

paused. "It was so cold and . . . I knew I couldn't make it out by myself. I'm just lucky you guys heard me yelling."

Kenny looked down at his hands in his lap. It was quiet, except for the howling wind rippling the tent.

Jason broke the silence. "Hey, guys, that's it! I think we should call our team 'The Songbird Expedition.' We're going to make it too. We're going to make it through the shadow of Denali. And to the top."

Kelly and Frank nodded. Kenny gave the thumbs-up sign.

"It's perfect," Dean said.

View of south peak of Mt. McKinley

Steve McCutcheon

CHAPTER 5

Summit Fever

Another day at Windy Corner, and the weather finally cleared.

Jason dozed. He dreamed of spiking the football down hard at the end zone. Another touchdown.

He dreamed of Stephanie. Her smile. Her soft touch and golden blond hair.

"Jase!" Jason was jerked awake. It was his dad.

"Let's get moving! It's clear out here, and you can see for . . . "

Suddenly, they heard a deep rumble from above. They looked up to see a huge cloud of snow rolling down the mountain. It was like a gigantic wave.

Jason and his dad watched in awe. The cloud tumbled down, down, down. As the snow gathered speed, the rumble turned into a roar. It spilled to the bottom, and the cloud fanned out. Snow sprayed in all directions. The avalanche missed their camp by 100 feet.

"Whew!" Dean sighed. "Of all the climbs I've made on Denali, I've never been this close to an avalanche.

"We were lucky," he added. "The avalanche probably started because of the loose **snow pack** after the storm. Mother nature is a mighty force, isn't she?"

After the avalanche, the air turned quiet. Jason looked around. The jagged, snowcapped mountains loomed all around him. He felt small. Like a speck of life in a sky of snow.

Jason felt stiff all over. Too much time lying around.

He did leg kicks and squats to loosen up. Then a few dozen jumping jacks.

Jason was ready to climb. But they wouldn't be going anywhere for another 12 hours.

"We need to let the snow settle after the storm. Just to be safe," Dean announced. "Heavy snowfalls can turn these slopes into death traps."

Another day in the tent? Ugh.

Jason sat outside next to the snow blocks. He was proud of their work. The snow blocks had held up and blocked the wind. They were safe, for now, in their tiny home. High up on the mountain.

A light wind blew puffs of snow along the ground. Jason yawned. He wasn't really tired, but he often seemed to need more air.

He sucked a cold breath into his lungs. He could hardly believe he was on Denali. They were up so high!

Jason could see for miles and miles. Smaller snowcapped mountains below him. Blue glaciers coming out of jagged rock. Tundra that stretched in all directions.

Jason shivered. He headed back inside the tent to sleep. Or at least try to.

Inside the tent, Frank snored loudly. Jason zipped himself into his sleeping bag. He blew puffs of breath into the air, watching the steam rise. Inside his bag, he was warm. Warm in the cold, cold air of Denali.

The team moved swiftly the next day. They passed a huge crevasse. Then another.

Soon they were in an area that had dozens of large crevasses. The snow was stiff and crusty.

It was silent except for the crunching of snow under crampons. Looking down into the crevasses was eerie. Jason tried to concentrate on the trail directly under his feet.

The temperature was 10° above zero. Jason put his face mask on. Although the sun was shining brightly, the air was cold. It stung his cheeks.

The team trudged on. Five hundred feet higher, the weather began to change. Snowflakes tumbled out of the sky. The wind blew at 20 mph. The team stopped for food and drinks.

The wind picked up speed. Snow whipped up into swirls all around them.

Just after the team stopped, Frank fell to his knees. He was wearing only long underwear under his wind pants. His legs were freezing cold.

The other team members took off their packs. They formed a small windbreak for Frank. He knelt behind it to undress and put on pile pants.

The wind continued to blast, blowing snow in their faces. Jason looked over at his dad. Frank looked pale and weak. His breathing was hard and fast.

What if Dad doesn't make it? Jason thought. What if he dies on this stupid mountain? He brushed the thought away.

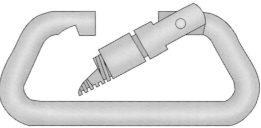

One style of carabiner

After food and drink, the team continued on. It became more and more difficult to breathe.

Jason's head pounded. His shoulders and back ached. He swallowed hard, pushing back panic. For the first time, he felt like quitting.

The team took a few steps into the blinding snow. Then they stopped to rest. A few more steps. Then rest. Their progress was slow and painful.

In the distance, Jason could see a small orange shape. Was it a tent?

He squinted his eyes. The blowing snow whirled around him.

"We're almost to 14.2," Dean said. "A couple of Park Service rangers camp here to carry out rescues. Hang in there, gang. We're almost there."

Just seeing the tent energized Jason. They would make it. As slow and sure as snails. But they would make it. Finally.

Jason dreaded setting up camp. He was too beat after hours of climbing.

But he pushed himself to do it. Just setting down the heavy pack was a relief. He knew as soon as camp was set up, he could rest. And sleep. The wind died to a mild whisper.

Dean announced a rest of two days. Maybe more depending on how everyone felt. No one complained. Except Kenny. He had summit fever. The higher they got, the more impatient he became. But Jason was grateful for the decision to camp.

"In the next couple days, Kenny and I will go back down to 13,000 feet. We'll bring up more supplies. In the meantime, you can rest, take some pictures, and just goof off," Dean said.

Jason grinned. He was glad he wouldn't be climbing back down. After climbing up, and back down, over and over again to cache supplies, this was a real treat! He could relax in the sun. His body surely needed it. His shoulders ached. But relief was on the way.

Jason spent a few hours sleeping. Then he aired out clothing and sleeping bags. He played cards with Kelly and reorganized gear.

He watched his dad closely. Frank was completely exhausted. After a meal of freeze-dried chicken and rice, he went directly to the tent. He slept all day and well into the night.

"Do you think they can hear Dad's snoring down on the Kahiltna?" Jason joked. Kelly laughed.

Kelly sat in the sun nursing a mild case of **trench foot.** Small blisters had formed on her toes. The skin was moist. She sprinkled on foot powder and wriggled her toes in the cold air.

"Good as new," Kelly muttered as she pulled on a fresh pair of socks.

The next day, Frank felt much better. His headache was gone. The extra time spent at 14,200 had helped him recharge.

THE DENALI MEDICAL RESEARCH PROJECT

From 1982 to 1989, the Denali Medical Research Project was set up at the 14,200 foot level of Denali. Each year, a doctor and his coworkers spent May and June at the camp. They studied **hypothermia, frostbite,** and how mountain sickness affects a climber's body.

In 1982, two Japanese climbers were saved after they took a bad fall at 16,000 feet. That same year, more than 100 people were treated for illness and injury. The camp not only helped scientists learn but saved people's lives as well.

Today, the medical camp is closed down due to lack of money. Park rangers still use the camp, however, as a base to conduct rescues during Denali's climbing season.

By late afternoon, Kenny and Dean had arrived. They cached some food and stove gas. Then they marked the mound of snow with wands.

The next morning, everyone was well rested.

"Songbird Expedition," Jason shouted. "Get ready to climb!"

Jason adjusted his crampons on his boots. The wind was blowing mildly. He layered on clothes—his wind suit on top. After a breakfast of instant oatmeal and hot chocolate, the team filled their water bottles.

Jason roped up behind Kelly. He liked being with her. She was thorough, yet carefree. He admired her a lot. Or maybe he had a crush on her.

The wind blew harder. Jason felt a pain in his chest when he took a deep breath. He turned to look at Kenny, who had ordered a rest break. Kenny took a bandanna out of his pack. He folded it and tied it around his head. A flap of fabric covered his mouth.

"My lungs hurt when I breathe," Kenny said. "This will keep the heat in."

The next 1,000 feet were slow going. Kelly and Frank had minor headaches. Even Dean felt a little sick to his stomach.

The climb from 14,200 feet up was definitely harder. Dean was concerned about mountain sickness. Headaches can be an early warning sign. So he insisted on moving even slower.

"Okay, folks. We need to take another rest stop," Dean ordered. "Time to eat and drink."

"Even if you don't . . . feel like it," Jason chimed in. He could now predict what Dean was going to say before he said it.

What a pain. Getting his water bottle out of his pack was annoying. He had to take off his bulky overmitts. Then his mittens. He had to unzip his pack and dig around for his snacks. Half the time, the zipper would stick from the cold.

Jason's fingers felt numb. He tried to get his snacks and water out quickly. But his hands froze in the chilling air.

He struggled to warm them again by putting them under his armpits. He would rather just skip all these rest breaks.

But Dean warned them every day. "You have to eat and drink even when you don't feel like it. Climb very slowly so your body gets used to the thin air. Patience is the key. Blah, blah, blah . . ."

Kenny helped Kelly melt snow on the stoves. Each climber filled his water bottle, adding spiced cider powder.

Jason's bottle was insulated. But this high up, everything froze . . . eventually.

He drank the hot liquid slowly. He savored every warm sip.

"Can you believe it? We've been on the mountain almost two weeks. All I can think of is the summit," Jason said. But no one felt like talking.

Jason was in a good mood. And so was Denali.

It was clear and cold. A bright sunny day. Jason thought he

was getting used to the cold. Or maybe he had just forgotten what warm air felt like.

"We're coming up on the fixed-rope section," Dean explained. "The steepest part of the climb—from 15 to 16,000 feet."

Jason looked around. A steep wall of hard-packed snow and ice lay before him. Across the wall, a fixed rope was bolted into the snow.

"The fixed rope is for safety," Dean said. "In case anyone falls. It was placed here by other climbers for all to use."

One style of jumar ascender

Jason remembered practicing on a fixed line back on the Kahiltna. But now they were doing it for real. He was nervous. He took a deep breath to calm himself.

Jason attached a carabiner to the front of his harness. The carabiner was attached by a short rope to a **jumar ascender.** The jumar then clipped into the fixed rope.

"The jumar can only move forward, not backward," Dean said. "So if you fall, it will immediately grip the rope and hold your weight.

"Remember to **self-arrest** if you have to," Dean continued. "Dig your ice ax into the snow to stop your fall. But of course, nobody's going to fall. Right?"

Jason felt nervous. He looked around. Dean led the group. Kelly was in the rear.

One step at a time, they climbed. Jason looked down. One thousand feet of sheer ice tumbled down below him. If someone fell . . .

No, Jason thought. No negative thoughts.

Jason took each step carefully, digging his crampons into

the ice. He planted his ice ax with each step too. It served as a good walking stick, helping him keep his balance.

Jason looked straight ahead. He concentrated on each step.

The climb seemed to take forever. Jason liked being roped up with all the others. The rope was like a shared lifeline.

But what if they fell? Wouldn't the weight of a few yank them all off the mountain?

Jason tried to clear his mind of such thoughts. He struggled to stay focused on each step.

Finally, they reached the end of the fixed rope. What relief! Jason removed his backpack.

"Songbird Expedition," Jason shouted. "We made it!" Everyone looked tired but happy.

"Now we need to cache some supplies," Dean said. "And remember, dig deep. We've got company." Dean pointed to a raven flying overhead.

The climbers took their time eating, drinking, and resting. The climb back down was fast and fun.

CHAPTER  6

To the Top

The next day, the weather turned foggy. With cloud cover, the air was warmer.

Jason was more confident on the second climb up the fixed rope. The first climb had made for a long day. Climbing up. Digging a cache. Ten hours for the total carry.

Today, they were climbing a little faster. Summit fever was contagious. Jason felt Kenny's push to go faster.

The view from 16,000 feet was spectacular. Jason could see the black rocks of the North Peak. Yawning glaciers followed by wide-open tundra.

It was hard to believe, but here he was. Close to the top of Denali. The highest mountain in all of North America.

Would they make it to the summit? After all this work, would they finally make it?

Jason looked at his dad. Frank's headache was back. Only worse. He had made it up the fixed line. But he had stumbled on the way back down to bring up more supplies.

Still, Frank insisted on moving ahead. Jason admired his willpower. But he was worried too.

Light snow began to fall. Jason got into a rhythm. Breathe deep. Take a step. Breathe deep. The snow below his feet turned soft and mushy.

Jason kept an eye on his dad. He was breathing heavily.

Then Jason saw his dad fall to his knees. But slowly, Frank heaved himself back up. He was very pale.

"Here, Dad," Jason said. "Have a drink." Jason stopped and pulled out his water bottle. He also pulled a hunk of frozen banana bread from his pocket.

"No, I'm not hungry," Frank said. "Just a little rest and I'll be okay."

"Frank, you've got to eat," Dean ordered. "We'll set up camp here," he announced to the others. "And take another 24-hour rest. Just to be safe."

Everyone agreed. Except Kenny. His summit fever was getting worse. He wanted to push on. But he was outnumbered.

Frank sat propped against two backpacks while the rest of the team set up camp.

"Once we hit 17,200 feet, there's no more caching. From 17.2, we go for the summit," Dean said.

"Or we don't," he added. "It all depends on the weather. And how we're doing."

It was snowing harder. The temperature dropped to 10° below zero.

Jason shivered inside the tent. He finished reading his murder mystery. The story took him away from the mountain. Away from his tiredness.

His dad lay next to him, exhausted. Occasionally, Frank coughed. A dry, raspy cough.

For dinner, they had freeze-dried beef Stroganoff and sweet-and-sour chicken. Then peanut butter cups, spiced cider, and hot chocolate followed. Everyone ate at least two dinners.

Frank wouldn't eat. Jason knew something was wrong. Terribly wrong.

"Here, Dad, eat some chocolate," Jason said. He held it close to Frank's mouth.

"I said I'm not hungry," Frank snapped.

Jason begged him to eat. But Frank refused. He was weak, but he could still argue.

"I'll be okay," he said. "Just give me some time." Frank stumbled out of the tent. Jason followed.

Frank coughed hard. His lungs made a raspy, muffled sound.

Dean walked up. "Listen, Frank," Dean said. "You're too weak to keep climbing. You've got serious mountain sickness. We've got to get you down while you're still able to walk."

"No!" Frank said angrily. "I can make it. Let me rest awhile. I'll be okay."

Jason was crushed. He knew his dad was not making sense. Frank wasn't going to make the summit. Worse still, he might die up here.

Jason knew the remedy for mountain sickness. Down. Go down to lower altitudes as soon as possible. Before you pass out . . . and die.

Jason felt his dad's disappointment down deep. So deep that he wasn't sure he wanted to make the summit. Not without his dad.

At last, Frank agreed. He wasn't going to reach the summit. His life was in danger.

Slowly, Frank sipped from Jason's water bottle. He coughed loudly between swigs.

"Dad," Jason said. "I'm not going up either. Not without you. I can't do it without you."

Frank looked up at him. His face was worn, but his eyes still looked bright and hopeful.

"It's your decision. But I don't think you should give up. Not because of me. Walk through your fears, Jason. You're still strong. And you've come this far. I know you can do it . . ." Frank's voice trailed off.

Jason couldn't decide. A part of him wanted to quit. Another part of him wanted to keep going. Go for the summit.

Jason looked all around him. The whole world was at his feet.

Denali was a place of breathless beauty. It could also be a cold, brutal place. But at the same time, it was the most majestic place in the world.

Jason breathed deep. I'm going to go for it, he thought. For me and for Dad. I can't give up now. "Songbird Expedition . . . to the summit," Jason said quietly.

Jason's dad forced a smile. They hugged long and hard.

"Good luck, son," Frank whispered.

Jason helped his dad organize his pack. He knew the sooner they got down, the better.

"Don't worry, Jason," Dean said. "With food, rest, and a lower **elevation,** he should be fine. As long as we act now. We'll eat, rest, and then start our way down," Dean finished.

"The team is now under Kelly's direction," Dean said to the others. "Remember, go slowly. And above all, play it safe."

The next day, the Songbird Expedition awoke to fair skies. Jason stayed roped up between Kelly and Kenny. At times, he felt scared and alone. He missed his dad.

At other times, he felt bold. Strong.

Don't give up. That's what his dad always said. Face your dangers. Walk through your fears. Make the summit.

The snow was wind-hardened. Jason stomped each boot into its crisp surface.

The climbers moved slowly. Jason breathed deep—as deep as he could. More air. He counted his breaths to pass the time.

The climb to 17,200 feet took five hours.

They were one day's climb from the summit. They had three days' worth of food, just in case. In case Denali was in a bad mood. The mighty mountain always had the final say.

Jason looked up at Denali's summit. Dark clouds loomed overhead.

"Stormy weather is coming our way," Kelly said. "And you know what that means."

Jason dreaded the backbreaking job of building tent walls. But it was necessary. A blizzard up this high could yank a tent out of the snow. Batter everyone to death.

After wanding the camp and unroping, they dug deep into the snow and set up the tent. Then they built a wall.

By midnight, the snow was blowing sideways. Jason peeked outside the tent. He couldn't see up or down. Another whiteout.

The wind beat the tent, blowing snow in every direction. It whistled and howled. The tent rattled and shook. The temperature dropped to 25° below zero.

Jason couldn't feel his toes. He remembered what Kelly had warned earlier. "If you don't feel your feet, you may think they're all right. But the truth is, they could be frostbitten."

It was hard getting his feet out of his boots. His toes were swollen and cold. He rubbed them in his hands to get back some feeling.

Kenny lifted his parka and put Jason's toes on his stomach. "This ought to do the trick," Kenny said.

The three of them sat in the tent waiting. Hours passed and the wind didn't let up. Its force was as strong as a hurricane. The wind whipped the tent violently and ripped it at the seams.

Jason moved around, trying to exercise his arms and legs. But they were so cramped it was hard to move.

The storm raged on. Jason felt his stomach growl. He was hungry and thirsty.

They had eaten five hours ago. But the bitter cold was draining him. He felt weak and frightened. We could die in this tent, Jason thought.

How long can this go on? What if we're trapped here for days? Jason knew it was possible. Other climbers had died in storms just like this one. He started to feel suffocated. Trapped. Like the walls were caving in on him.

I've got to distract my mind, he thought. Think of something positive.

Jason took off his overmitts. The cold stung his fingers. He wrestled with the zipper on his pack. It stuck. Then gave way.

Jason pulled out a book. It was the one Stephanie had given him before the climb.

He flipped through the pages, then stopped. There, pressed between the pages, was a pale blue flower. A forget-me-not. Smooth green leaves were pressed around the petals.

"Look, you guys! Green!" Jason exclaimed. "We haven't seen anything green for almost two weeks."

Kenny and Kelly smiled faintly.

Jason sighed. He didn't have the energy to read. Not here. Not now.

Before closing the book, Jason glanced down at the pages. There in bold lettering he read a single quote:

Kites fly highest against the wind, not with it.

Jason closed the book. We'll make it, he thought. We'll make it through this storm. We've just got to . . .

The three climbers huddled close together in their sleeping bags. Outside, the storm raged. They huddled closer, trying to keep in the heat. The wind continued to wail.

Jason felt so weak and battered, he hardly moved. Finally, he fell asleep, wedged tightly between Kelly and Kenny.

❖⌁❖⌁❖

When Jason awoke, Kelly and Kenny were gone. The air was quiet. He heard voices outside the tent.

"This is it," Kelly said. "Clear skies. Time for our final push."

Had he heard her right? Clear skies? They made it through the storm?

No, he wasn't dreaming. Jason sat up. Hunger pangs bit at his stomach.

After breaking camp and eating a huge breakfast, they roped up. It was a cold day. A few degrees below zero. But no wind.

The snow crunched beneath their feet. Jason felt safe in the middle position on the rope.

His legs and neck felt stiff. Maybe from all the lying around, he thought. He felt better once his muscles warmed.

They continued climbing, reaching Denali Pass. The pass was often like a wind tunnel but not today. They were lucky.

The pass was quiet, almost eerie. They slowed their pace. Every step of the way was hard. Jason's breathing was shallow and quick. It became an effort to talk. They trudged along in silence.

Before long, Jason's head pounded. He felt like he couldn't breathe. With each step, he had to stop and take three breaths. He couldn't seem to get enough air in his lungs no matter how deeply he breathed. His body shook.

Maybe I can't really do this, he thought. Doubt crept into his mind.

Then Kelly turned and made a time-out sign. Jason was relieved. He cheered to himself.

"So far, so good," Kelly announced. "But we've got to eat . . . and drink. We can't . . ." Her words were broken by breaths. ". . . blow it now."

"Not this close!" Kenny said. "We're almost there. We've got to . . . take advantage of this . . . clear weather. Before it's . . . too late."

"We can't take . . . any . . . chances," Kelly added, sternly. "Slow down and . . . eat."

Kelly had the last word, and Jason was relieved. Although he could almost taste the summit, his pack was heavy. And his legs felt like rubber. He was getting too close to exhaustion to keep going.

One style of ice ax

The sun appeared from behind the shadows of the pass. It was still close to zero degrees. But the sun's rays energized them.

Jason could see the summit. He felt a rush of energy. Now he had summit fever. All he wanted was to stand on the summit of Denali. The mighty, majestic Denali.

Slowly, they climbed south. They headed towards a broad ridge known as the Football Field. A long flat, open area at 19,600 feet.

Another rest stop. Jason dropped his pack and fell to the ground. He didn't say a word. The thin, cold air made breathing difficult.

They ate granola bars and drank more water. So close . . . and yet so far away.

Jason was dying to run the rest of the way and be done with it. Only a couple hundred yards. A couple of football fields. He could handle it.

But his body wouldn't let him. Although his mind said "go," his body said "slow." One exhausting step at a time.

Crossing the Football Field, Jason felt his knees buckle under him. He stumbled several times.

The climbers stopped to rest every few steps. In his mind, Jason kept repeating, You can do it. You can do it.

It was like going for a touchdown in slow motion. Everything was in slow motion. His movements. His speech.

Jason felt like he was caught in a vacuum. Inside a sealed container without air.

He looked up into the deep blue sky. He felt so small. Like a tiny bug struggling in a swift current.

At the end of the Football Field, the three of them hugged. It was then that he knew they would make it. Make it together.

Either all of them would make it or none of them would. · That's the way it was. Jason could feel it in his bones.

One more ridge to climb to 20,000 feet. Denali stood majestically waiting, waiting.

Jason's excitement grew. He dug his crampons into the hard-packed snow. Each step was planned, thought out. And every breath too.

The team neared the summit. Only a hundred more feet.

Jason felt great happiness as he planted his ice ax at the top of the world. He jumped into the air with joy. He was there. On the summit.

Slowly, Jason turned in a circle. What a beautiful view! The heartland of Alaska stretching all the way out to the ocean. Rivers and lakes snaking their way through the tundra. Snowcapped peaks and blue glaciers. And he was standing above them all!

"Oh, what a beautiful planet," Kenny exclaimed. He took out a small Alaskan flag and stuck it into the snow.

Kelly pulled a CB radio from her pack. "Jason, why don't you check on your father?" she suggested.

Jason turned the knob on the radio. "Ten four, this is the Songbird Expedition. Standing atop the tallest mountain in North America. Do you copy?"

"Congratulations, son. I knew you could do it," Frank replied. "It's one heck of a way to celebrate your sixteenth birthday!"

"My birthday!" Jason cried. "I forgot all about it!

"Thanks, Dad," Jason continued. "You were right. I <u>could</u> do it. And I did. I did!"

After ten joyous minutes at the top, it was time to head down. Lenticular clouds were quickly moving in from the west. Kelly took a few pictures. Then the climbers started their **descent.**

"Remember, we need to be careful," Kelly warned. "Most accidents happen on the way down."

∻Ș∻Ș∻

It took them two days to reach the Kahiltna Glacier. Clear skies brought the glacier pilot in right on schedule.

∻Ș∻Ș∻

After two and a half weeks on the mountain, Jason was glad to be home. He found himself thinking about things he hadn't noticed before. He noticed his mother's spring flowers—green and yellow and blue. He noticed the smell of cottonwood buds, sweet in the summer breeze.

Jason stood on the green grass of home and looked up. Tall, cold Denali sliced the blue sky.

It's another world up there, Jason thought. Mighty Denali. A world where nothing grows, except the heart and soul of the climber.

Appendix

Food

Climbing in cold weather burns lots of calories. Climbers work extremely hard, pulling sleds with gear and carrying their backpacks to the summit.

Climbers may not feel like eating. This feeling comes from climbing at high altitudes. But it is necessary for them to eat even when they don't feel like it.

Climbers need from 4,000 to 6,000 calories per day. The following is a list of foods climbers should pack for Denali:

        bagels and cream cheese

        candy bars

        canned meat and fish

        cheddar cheese

        coffee, tea, and hot chocolate

        frozen vegetables

        gorp (raisins and peanuts)

        instant oatmeal

        instant soup

        Kool-Aid (to add to water bottles for variety)

        rice and pasta

Often the team will prepare a one-pot meal, a "glop pot," where many foods are combined in one pot. A stew of meat, rice, vegetables, cheddar cheese, and noodles is delicious after a long, hard day of climbing.

After the team caches their sleds and snowshoes (at the 11,000- to 14,000-foot levels), freeze-dried foods are used. From this point on, the climbers travel light.

Freeze-dried dinners are prepackaged and weigh only about 4 oz. They are prepared by dropping a pouch in heated water. Freeze-dried dinners come in many varieties: beef Stroganoff, macaroni and cheese, sweet-and-sour chicken, black beans and rice, and more.

Climbers plan for 17 to 25 days of food for each person when climbing the West Buttress of Denali. Most climbers also cache six days of food and fuel at the Kahiltna Glacier at 7,200 feet.

The Kahiltna is the drop-off and pickup point for the climbers. Poor weather often delays the glacier pilot for several days. Climbers need the cached food and supplies while waiting to get off the mountain in bad weather.

Clothing

For footwear, climbers often wear plastic double boots. These boots have a plastic outer shell and an inner boot made of foam or felt. They are quite warm and light.

Climbers wear two pairs of light socks and one or two pairs of heavy wool socks.

Climbers must air out their feet every night and change the inner socks often. If the feet are too moist, blisters will form from rubbing inside the boot. This is called trench foot.

It is best to layer clothing when climbing. Climbers can remove a top layer if they get too hot. Or add a layer if they get too cold.

Long underwear made of a fabric called polypropylene is best. The fabric dries very fast. It draws moisture away from the skin. So when climbers sweat, they don't get damp.

For the next layer, climbers wear a wool sweater or shirt covered by a pile jacket. Pile is a soft, velvety fabric. On top of the pile jacket, a parka is worn.

Parkas are big, light coats that are very warm. The best ones have lots of pockets with zippers. Climbers use the pockets for film, sunscreen, a pocket knife, lip balm, and chocolate bars.

A wind jacket and wind pants are put on last. These are used during extreme storm conditions when the wind is very strong. The wind suit is also useful during wet snowfalls.

At 8,000 feet, climbers may wear only their long underwear on hot, sunny days. The snow reflects the sun's heat. These days are known as "T-shirt days."

At 20,000 feet, however, the temperature may reach 30° below zero. Climbers must layer clothing, including wind suits.

For headgear, a wool ski hat works well in moderate temperatures. But when it gets very cold, climbers wear face masks to keep their cheeks and foreheads from freezing.

Lightweight gloves may be layered with wool gloves to keep the climbers' hands warm. Thick nylon overmitts are worn on top of the wool gloves for extra warmth. Climbers remove the overmitts to zip zippers and remove items from their packs.

During blizzard conditions, ski goggles are worn over the face mask. Snow blindness can be a problem for climbers. It is caused by sun reflecting off the snow and hurting the eyes. A good pair of glacier goggles can prevent snow blindness.

Climbing Equipment

The use of good equipment is a must when climbing Denali. It is important to use a large backpack that is comfortable and fits well. Climbers carry 30 to 50 pounds of gear in their backpacks.

A seat harness made of nylon webbing is worn around the climber's bottom and thighs. In front, the harness is cinched together with a carabiner.

A climbing rope is used to connect the climbers together. The rope is attached to each climber's harness. This safety measure is very important. If a climber falls through a crevasse, he is still connected. Then he can be hauled out by the others.

Some climbers use a chest harness as well. It fits around the shoulders and fastens together in front with a carabiner. The chest harness prevents a climber from flipping upside down after falling into a crevasse.

A jumar ascender is a clamp that slides up the climbing rope and grips it tightly. If a climber falls, the jumar immediately grips the rope and holds the climber's weight. It is used on steep ascents or climbing out of a hole.

Crampons are fastened onto boots to prevent slipping. Crampons dig in and provide traction when climbing on ice and hard-packed snow. Climbers call them "foot fangs."

Climbers may use snowshoes or skis to travel along glaciers. Snowshoes are safe and slow. Skiing is faster, but climbers must be very experienced.

When wearing snowshoes, climbers may use ski poles to keep their balance. The snowshoes and skis are cached somewhere between 11,000 and 14,000 feet. The rest of the climb is made with boots and crampons.

An ice ax is used for climbing snow and ice. The bottom of the handle has a metal spike and can be used as a walking stick. The top of the handle has a curved steel blade that can be thrust into the ice to anchor the climber. The ice ax is often tied to the harness so the climber can reach it easily.

Sleds are used to carry gear up to the 11,000- to 14,000-foot level. Flat-bottomed, plastic children's sleds work well. The sled is attached to the climber's harness or backpack by a long rope.

Snow shovels with large wide scoops are used for building snow walls around tents, digging into the snow to build a cache, and removing snow after an avalanche.

A portable camping stove is used to melt snow and cook meals. It is fueled by white gas. One stove is enough for three people.

Wands are tall, orange bamboo stakes used by climbers. Climbers place wands every 150 feet to mark their trail. If a whiteout occurs on the way back down, the climbers use the wands to find their way. Wands are also used to mark food caches and outline the area of a camp.

Some climbing teams take a CB radio so they can communicate with others. There is a radio caretaker on the Kahiltna Glacier at the height of climbing season. His job is to monitor the weather. He also communicates with the glacier pilots to get teams on and off the mountain.

Repair kits to fix broken equipment, maps, and first aid kits are also important items for climbers.

Hazards

Many risks are involved when climbing the tallest mountain in North America. Hiring a guide is one way to make for a safer climb. Guides provide leadership for the team.

The guides who climb Denali are experienced climbers. They know the mountain well. They know

- what equipment to bring
- how to treat mountain sickness
- how to proceed in a storm
- how to perform crevasse rescues
- first aid skills for the Arctic weather
- and how to build tent walls.

The mountain can be climbed in two ways—**expedition style** and alpine style. With expedition-style climbing, teams make carries of food and fuel up the mountain. They cache or bury the supplies. Then they climb back down to bring up more. Expedition style is a slow, safe way to climb.

With alpine style, climbers carry everything with them in a single push to the top. They take less food. There is a greater risk for mountain sickness with this style.

Besides mountain sickness, climbers are at risk for dehydration, exhaustion, frostbite, and hypothermia. A climber's body and mind must be well prepared.

Glossary

alpenglow the pink and golden hue seen on the mountaintops when the sun is setting or rising

alpine style a form of climbing where climbers carry all that they need in their backpacks rather than using sleds and caching supplies

altitude measurement of how high a landform is above the earth's surface

ascent the climb up a mountain

cache to store food and supplies; a safe place for storing food and supplies. Climbers dig caches in the snow to bury their supplies.

carabiner a metal hook much like a padlock. Climbers use carabiners to attach themselves to the climbing rope.

crampons metal spikes that are attached to climbing boots; foot fangs

crevasse a large crack or oblong hole in a glacier. A crevasse can be hundreds of feet deep.

crevasse field an area where there are many crevasses

dehydration when the body loses too much water

descent the climb down a mountain

elevation	height above the earth's surface
exhaustion	when a climber completely uses up his energy supply; state of being very tired
expedition style	a method of climbing where teams make carries of food and fuel up the mountain. They cache or bury the supplies and climb back down to bring up more. It is a slow, safe way to climb.
frostbite	the freezing of skin from extreme cold. When frostbite occurs, the skin becomes numb and pale.
glacier	a large mass of ice and snow
glop pot	a pot where many foods are cooked together to make a one-pot meal
gorp	a mixture of raisins and peanuts
hypothermia	condition where the body temperature drops below normal
jumar ascender	metal clamp that can be attached to the climbing rope. It will only slide forward and not backwards.
lenticular clouds	long, narrow curved clouds (in the shape of a lens) that signal very high winds
mountain sickness	(altitude sickness) illness that results when the body is unable to adjust to high altitudes

rockface	the surface of the rock that faces out
roped up	climbers are connected by a common rope, for safety reasons
self-arrest	stopping oneself in a fall
snow pack	the top layer of snow
summit	the top or highest point on a mountain
trench foot	condition that occurs when the feet stay wet and cold for a long period of time
tundra	the flat, treeless plains of the Arctic regions in Alaska
West Buttress of Denali	the climbing route up Denali from the west
whiteout	blowing, blinding snow that makes it impossible to see

Index

alpenglow, 25

alpine style, 8, 60

avalanche, 35–36, 59

caching, 8, 11, 22–23, 28–29, 40, 44–46, 56–57, 59–60

carabiner, 8, 10, 14, 37, 43, 58

chest harness, 10, 58

crampons, 8, 22, 29, 37, 40, 43, 54, 59

crevasse, 9–10, 12–14, 28, 33, 37, 58, 60

Denali, 5, 7–8, 16, 25, 28, 33, 35–36, 39, 41, 45, 48–49, 53–58, 60

Denali Medical Research Project, 39

Denali Pass, 6, 52

exhaustion, 28, 53, 60

expedition style, 60

Football Field, 6, 53–54

frostbite, 39, 60

hypothermia, 39, 60

jumar ascender, 43, 58

Kahiltna Glacier, 4–7, 39, 43, 55, 57, 59

Kahiltna Pass, 6, 20, 26

lenticular clouds, 24, 55

Motorcycle Hill, 6, 28

mountain sickness, 8, 26, 39, 41, 47, 60

Mt. McKinley (see Denali) 3–6, 17, 34

North Peak, 45

Ski Hill, 6, 19

skis, 5, 20, 22, 59

sleds, 8, 11, 14, 19, 22, 28–29, 56, 59

snowshoes, 8, 10–11, 20–23, 28, 30, 56, 59

trench foot, 39, 57

tundra, 30, 36, 45, 54

U.S. Park Service, 33, 38

West Buttress of Mt. McKinley, 5–6, 57

whiteout, 32, 50, 59

Windy Corner, 6, 32, 35